We All Share

GRANDPARENTS
AROUND THE WORLD

BY
PATRICIA LAKIN

BLACKBIRCH PRESS, INC.
WOODBRIDGE, CONNECTICUT

CONTENTS

Published by Blackbirch Press, Inc.
260 Amity Road
Woodbridge, CT 06525

e-mail: staff@blackbirch.com
website: www.blackbirch.com

©1999 Blackbirch Press, Inc.
First Edition

All rights reserved. No part of this book may be reproduced in any form without permission in writing from Blackbirch Press, Inc., except by a reviewer.

Printed in Singapore

10 9 8 7 6 5 4 3 2 1

Photo Credits
Cover: ©Robin Schwartz/International Stock Photo; Series logo, pp. 3, 5: ©Photodisc; pp. 7, 9 (bottom), 23, 29, 31 (bottom): ©Corel Corporation; p. 9 (top): ©Kate Bader/United Nations; p. 11: ©Ingeborg Lippmann/Peter Arnold, Inc.; p. 13, 21 (right): ©Martha Cooper/Peter Arnold, Inc.; p. 15: ©Jason Lauré; p. 17, 27 (right): ©Bill Wrenn/International Stock Photo; p. 21 (left): ©Bruce Glassman; p. 25: ©Chuck Haney; p. 27 (left): ©Doranne Jacobson/United Nations; p. 31 (top): ©Guillermo Aldana Espinosa/National Geographic.

Library of Congress Cataloging–in–Publication Data
Lakin, Patricia.
   Grandparents: around the world / by Patricia Lakin.
      p. cm.—(We all share)
   Includes bibliographical references and index.
   Summary: Examines the role grandparents play in various countries, including Iraq, Canada, the United States, China, Switzerland, Ecuador, and Italy, discussing their position as the elders in their cultures.
   ISBN 1-56711-146-7
      1. Grandparents—Cross-cultural studies—Juvenile literature. 2. Aged—Cross-cultural studies—Juvenile literature. [1. Grandparents. 2. Old age.] I. Title. II. Series.
HQ759.9.L34   1999
305.874'5—dc20   98-46854
                                                         CIP
                                                          AC

INTRODUCTION	3
UNITED STATES	4
RUSSIA	6
CHINA	8
IRAQ	10
CANADA	12
SWAZILAND	14
ECUADOR	16
ITALY	18
CYPRUS	20
SAUDI ARABIA	22
NATIVE AMERICAN	24
INDIA	26
ISRAEL	28
MEXICO	30
GLOSSARY	32
FOR MORE INFORMATION	32
INDEX	32

INTRODUCTION

If you are lucky, you will live to an old age. If you are very lucky, when you get old, you will be living in a family or a community that values the knowledge of its older members.

In most farm communities around the world, many people are needed to help with the daily chores. The more hands that help, the easier the chores become. Everyone from grandchildren to grandparents is expected to work. Any able-bodied person is a valued member in this community.

In some cultures, older people are not expected to work as hard as they did when they were young. Yet, elders are valued for their knowledge—it is often only they who understand important old traditions and can pass them down to future generations.

The special bond between grandparents and grandchildren allows knowledge and traditions to be passed down to new generations.

UNITED STATES

In the United States, looking and acting young is valued highly.

The United States is a country that celebrates youth. Most popular movies, magazines, and television shows feature young people. Being young and looking young is something that most Americans value.

In general, because of modern medicine and technology, life for the elderly is relatively good. There are even whole communities that have been designed especially for older citizens.

The majority of American families are nuclear instead of extended. A nuclear family is made up of

Many grandparents in the United States retire from work around age 60. This leaves them time for leisure activities and family visits.

parents and their children. An extended family can include grandparents, uncles, aunts, cousins, and other family members.

Because most American families are spread out, many older people in the United States do not live near their grandchildren. Luckily, traveling in the United States is fairly easy. Families often plan reunions and parties around holidays. In the summer, when most of the country has pleasant weather, many American families get together for picnics or barbecues. Many of these celebrations provide an excellent chance for several generations to see each other, catch up on family news, and enjoy one another's company.

RUSSIA

Many elderly citizens in Russia must work during their later years in order to afford daily basics.

Elder citizens of Russia have seen many changes in the land that was formerly known as The Soviet Union. Today, Russia is one of several states that belongs to a commonwealth (organized group of states or nations). Each state has individual cultural differences. Some states are more like Western Europe. Others are more like Middle Eastern countries.

Despite their differences, older people are treated in much the same way. Throughout the many states of the commonwealth, elderly men and women are still expected, and needed, to help with the daily routines of family life. Many play important roles in keeping their extended families together.

Older Russian men may gather to play chess, a favorite Russian game. Many older Russian women spend their days caring for their grandchildren or doing household chores, while their own adult children are away at work. Other elderly Russian women need to earn extra money because the pensions that they get from the government don't provide them with enough money to buy daily necessities. Many elderly women earn money by sweeping the streets or keeping the magnificent Russian subways clean.

Many elderly Russian women sweep streets to earn extra income during their later years.

CHINA

In China, community responsibility and respect come with age.

China, like other Asian countries, holds its older people in very high regard. Chinese elders are considered the wisest people of the community. Many elders in China are also seen as the heads of the families.

In many villages, towns, or neighborhoods in China, the elder men and women are also regarded as the community leaders. They are often the ones called upon to watch over and monitor the behavior of the younger generations.

Today, keeping strong and healthy is an important value for Chinese men and women—especially the elderly. Throughout all parts of China, in the early morning hours, elderly citizens can be seen standing erect, moving silently and gracefully. They are practicing an ancient form of Chinese exercise called Tai ji quan, or Tai Chi, as it is called in the West. While these exercises may look simple, they work and stretch many muscles in the entire body. Tai ji quan also exercises the mind because it takes a great deal of concentration to perform.

Above: The elderly in China are often considered the guardians of the young.
Below: People of all ages practice Tai Chi in China's public places.

IRAQ

In Iraq, the religion of Islam teaches that wisdom comes with age.

Iraq is a Muslim country in the Middle East. The majority of Iraqis practice a religion called Islam. Part of the religious beliefs focus on the importance of family and family loyalty. Another aspect of their religion teaches Iraqis to have a great deal of respect for their elders. They strongly believe that wisdom comes with age.

Whether they live in the modern capital of Baghdad or a rural farming village, Iraqis treat their parents and grandparents with loyalty and respect.

Iraqi grandparents are usually the ones to pass on family history and traditions. One such tradition is the art of storytelling. Iraqis are famous for their great ability to captivate listeners with rich folklore.

Ancient crafts, such as traditional decorative metalwork, are passed down from elders to younger generations.

And in this busy society, it is most likely Iraqi grandparents who have the time to entertain their grandchildren with a wonderful tale. Young and old generations may sit down together to delight in the world-famous Iraqi story collection *The Arabian Nights' Entertainment*, also known as *The Thousand and One Nights*. In these tales, children learn about the fantastic adventures of Sinbad, the famous sailor from Baghdad.

CANADA

Learning survival skills from the community elders is an age-old Inuit tradition.

The Inuits live in the most northern part of Canada. These native people have settled along the coasts of the Arctic, Pacific, and Atlantic oceans. Some have settled along the shores of Baffin and Hudson bays. The Inuits have always used these bodies of water to find their major sources of food. They have fished for salmon and hunted for whales.

Although the Inuits of today still catch their food, the methods are very different than the ways of the past. Sadly, the older Inuits may be the only ones left who can teach the hunting skills of long ago. These ancient skills were once key for survival in this cold climate.

Inuit village men used to fish for salmon through holes in the ice. Or, they would go out in hand-made boats, called umiaks, and use harpoons to spear and catch whales. When these men, or entire families, needed to travel across the ice-covered land, they used sleds that were pulled by specially trained dog teams. All these things—from salmon fishing to boat making to trekking across a barren land—required special skills. They also required special knowledge. But this is not the kind of knowledge one can get from books. This knowledge can only be passed from one generation to another.

Today, fishing boats are used to catch salmon. The whales are no longer hunted. And the dog sleds have been replaced by snowmobiles. But deep within the Inuit culture there remains a basic respect for age. It is understood that only the older generations hold the key to unlocking the ways of the past.

An Inuit grandmother teaches her granddaughter the art of traditional handicrafts.

SWAZILAND

The young people of Swaziland are taught to honor and help the elders of their communities.

Swaziland is a small country in the southeastern part of Africa. It is sandwiched between the Republic of South Africa and Mozambique.

Like so many small countries, Swaziland once had its own traditional way of life. The elders are needed to help keep the ancient traditions alive. But these old practices are not the only way of life young Swazis know. Western culture has influenced them. They see what life is like in Western society by watching television and movies. Despite other influences, the Swazi elders still maintain strong control over the younger generations.

In turn, younger Swazis know it is their responsibility to care for their elders. Older Swazi men and women do not have to worry about their own welfare. They are assured that their children will care for them if they should get sick, or become too weak to care for themselves.

To make sure that young Swazi children will continue to show respect for their elders, each Swazi boy joins a youth group. The group consists of boys the same age. In the group, they learn how to show proper respect for older generations. They also learn to honor the Swazi tradition of libbutfo, which means helping each other whenever it is necessary.

Many elderly people in Swaziland work in the crafts industry, where knowledge of traditional ways is most helpful. Here, a woman brings bundles of newly dyed grass to be used in woven items.

ECUADOR

The government of Ecuador does much to take care of the country's elderly citizens.

Ecuador is the smallest country in South America. The equator runs through it and gives the country its name—*Ecuador* is the Spanish word for equator.

Like many other South Americans, Ecuadorians show a great deal of respect for their elders. Whether elders live in cities or rural mountain towns, they know many skills that are important for the younger generations to learn. Some Ecuadorian children living in the mountains may have a grandparent teach them crafts such as basket-weaving, or how to weave wool cloth from a loom.

Ecuador has both a large rural and a large city population. But, no matter where older Ecuadorians live, they know that other family members will be strong support for them.

The Ecuadorian government has also provided a form of social security for its citizens. That means that the older generation knows they will get a pension and medical care. With money and good health benefits guaranteed, Ecuadorian elders know that they will be well cared for.

A grandmother takes her granddaughter for a walk in downtown Quito, the capital of Ecuador.

ITALY

Extended families are common in Italy, and grandparents are often caregivers for the youngest generation.

Italy is a European country that juts out into the Mediterranean Sea. Like many other people in this region, Italians look upon their family as the most important factor in their lives. Elder Italians and grandparents are treated with great respect and loyalty. If the elder members of a family are unable to work or care for themselves, younger members are always expected to help.

In many instances, grandparents will live with their grown children and kids. Both parents can go off to work knowing that their kids are being well cared for. If the grandparents do not live in the same house with their children and grandchildren, parents still encourage strong relationships between the youngest and oldest generations. Italian parents know that older generations have a wealth of knowledge and traditions to pass on to their children.

One such tradition is teaching younger Italians how to make pasta the traditional way—by hand, not by machine. This process takes many hours. Family recipes are handed down from one generation to the next. Young and old agree, there isn't a pasta machine that can beat the taste of pasta made the old-fashioned way!

Italian grandparents often pass on the secrets of making traditional foods. Here, an elderly man puts his home-grown grapes in a wine press.

CYPRUS

Cyprus is a tiny island nation in the Mediterranean, off the coast of Greece.

Cyprus is a small island country in the eastern part of the Mediterranean Sea. Like many other Mediterranean peoples, Cypriots value their families, and show them respect and loyalty.

The government in Cyprus has passed laws that reinforce those same values. Elderly Cypriots are given good free medical care. They also know that the pensions they receive from the government will let them live comfortable lives, even though they may no longer work.

In their retirement years, with the government social security program, elder Cypriots can spend time with friends, family, and grandchildren. Men

Above: During their retirement years, many grandparents spend a great deal of time with their grandchildren.
Right: Pottery making is an age-old craft in Cyprus, handed down from generation to generation.

can be found at local cafes, chatting with friends and drinking coffee. Women also spend time with friends, but usually visiting at one another's homes. Some of their free time is also spent teaching their grandchildren an age-old Cypriot craft—making pottery.

SAUDI ARABIA

Preserving and passing along the old Saudi traditions is the special job of the elders.

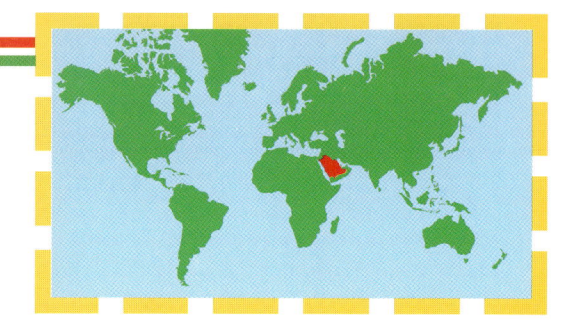

Saudi Arabia is a Muslim country rich in oil. Most of the people follow the Islamic faith. Their religion instructs them to show respect and loyalty to their elders. It is part of every Saudi's belief to treat their grandparents and other elders with great respect. Elders are regarded as the wisest members of the community.

Today, young Saudi's know that their grandparents are the ones who know the ways of Saudi life that existed before oil was discovered in 1938.

Before oil, Riyadh—Saudi's modern capital city—was a walled area built from mud bricks. Today, glass and steel high-rise buildings tower above the hot, flat desert country.

Many customs and traditions in Saudi Arabia have not changed for centuries. It is the role of the elder citizens to teach grandchildren those customs. For example, different behaviors are expected from boys and girls. Men and women do not socialize together. This is true when they are young and old.

Since 1938, many Westerners have come to Saudi Arabia. These outsiders have brought their own influences and culture to many Saudi cities. Today, preserving the old ways alongside the new is the special job of the elders.

The males of an extended Saudi family gather to celebrate at a wedding.

NATIVE AMERICAN

In many Native American tribes, elders are called upon to settle disputes and to offer advice.

The Crow are Native Americans whose home is on the Great Plains of Montana.

It is the Crow tradition to look to parents, grandparents, and elders for guidance and wisdom. Elders are called upon to settle disputes among members of the tribe. Traditionally, the Crow had no definite rules about the roles people should play in their community. They applied this belief to the men, women, and elderly alike. Each individual was judged by what he or she did best. A woman who was a good hunter and rider was allowed to ride with the men. Men who were better at skinning and making clothing were allowed to do that job. Similarly, an elderly person who was a leader had to show that his or her position was deserved.

Today, there are over 8,000 Crow living on their reservation in Montana. Loyalty to the immediate and extended family is still valued. The elderly Crow are still held in high regard. They are considered teachers for the younger generation. But more importantly, the elderly Crow are the tribe's link with traditions and crafts practiced in the past.

Crow elders are relied upon to keep their heritage alive by teaching younger generations about rituals and traditions.

INDIA

Large extended families are common in India, and grandparents share a special bond with the young.

India is a huge country in Asia that juts out into the Indian Ocean. There are three major religions and many different languages.

Despite the variety of its people, Indians all over the country greatly value family relationships. Family loyalty is strong. Parents—especially mothers—spend a great deal of time and energy raising their children. In return, when the parents become elderly, they expect to be cared for by their children.

Caring for the elderly has been a long-standing tradition in India. As a result, there are no senior citizen homes in this country. Parents often live with the family of one of their grown children. Because of this, there are many adults living under one roof that can care for, teach, and entertain the children. Many grandparents have more time to spend with the youngsters than parents do. As a result, children and their grandparents develop very strong bonds. One common way they spend free time together is going to the movies. This pastime is the most popular activity in India!

Right: Grandmothers are commonly left to look after the young children in an Indian family.
Below: An elderly priest reads to his grandson.

ISRAEL

Israeli grandparents are an important source of history for younger generations as well as teachers of culture.

Israel is a relatively new state in the Middle East. It was created in 1948 as a permanent homeland for the Jewish people. There were Jewish settlers who came to the land much earlier, as well. As a result, a large number of Israel's Jewish elderly have come from other countries. The older citizens brought their foods, customs, cultures, and languages to their new land.

One of the things that grandparents may do with Israeli grandchildren is pass on their own personal histories and customs from their former homelands.

One Israeli child may learn about Poland before World War II. Another may learn about Russia before the war. And while Hebrew is the official language of the country, some youngsters may learn another language from their grandparents—Polish, Russian, or perhaps the language spoken by many Eastern European Jews: Yiddish.

The rituals and traditions of Jewish life are taught to the young by community elders. Here, a young Jewish boy learns the meaning of a Passover seder from his grandfather.

MEXICO

For many rural communities in Mexico, elders continue to lend a hand with work as long as they are able.

Mexico is bordered by the Gulf of Mexico on the east and by the Pacific Ocean on the west. Many village dwellers in this country have farm-based jobs, working with the land and the sea.

Mexico has several very modern cities, but there are also many small villages. In these villages, people often live simple lives—fishing or farming, or doing a bit of both. For the elderly Mexicans who live in these village communities, work continues throughout their entire lives.

Mexican village elders are respected because they are considered to be the heads of the family. They are also the younger generation's link with the past. They most often live with their children, grandchildren, and other family members. On Sunday, Mexican grandparents may take their grandchildren for services at a small Catholic church in the town square. Afterwards, grandparents, parents, and grandchildren may go to a nearby small town to watch a favorite Mexican sport—bullfighting. Many of Mexico's most famous bullfighters come from families of bullfighters. Their skills have been learned from the parents and grandparents that came before them.

Top: A squash ceremony in central Mexico. In rural regions, where centuries-old traditions are still a part of daily life, elders are expected to lead the ceremonies.
Above: An elderly woman weaves using traditional methods and tools.

GLOSSARY

Culture the ideas, traditions, customs, and way of life of a group of people.

Equator An imaginary line around the middle of Earth, halfway between the North and South poles.

Generation the descendents of a shared ancestor.

Loyal faithful to one's country, family, or beliefs.

Pension an amount of money paid regularly to a person who has retired.

Reservation an area of land set aside by government for a special purpose.

Rural to do with the countryside.

Technology the use of science and engineering to do practical things.

FOR MORE INFORMATION

Books

Families Around the World (series). Chatham, NJ: Raintree/Steck Vaughn.

Hausherr, Rosemarie. *Celebrating Families.* New York, NY: Scholastic Trade, 1997.

Smith, Debbie. *Israel: The Culture* (Lands, People & Culture). New York, NY: Crabtree Publications, 1998.

Westheimer, Ruth K. Pierre A. Lehu. Tracey Campbell Pearson (Photographer). *Dr. Ruth Talks About Grandparents: Advice For Making the Most of a Special Relationship.* New York, NY: Farrar Straus & Giroux, 1997.

Web Site

The Genealogy Home Page
Links to pages where you can search for your ancestors' records—www.genhomepage.com/full.html.

INDEX

Bullfighting, 31
Caftans, 7
Crow, 24–25
  reservation, 25
Extended family, 5, 6
Farming, 30
Fishing, 12, 30
Hunting, 12
Inuit, 12–13
Islam, 10, 22
Judaism, 28–29
Libbutfo, 15
Movies, 26
Muslim, 10
Nuclear family, 5
Passover, 29
Pasta, 19
Pension, 7, 20
Pottery, 21
Seder, 29
Social roles, 25
Social Security, 17, 20
Storytelling, 11
Tai Chi, *See* Tai ji quan.
Tai ji quan, 9
Turbans, 7
Umiaks, 13
World War II, 29
Yiddish, 29